Transformation

Transformation © Copyright 2019 by Dr. Shirley Hughes

Cover design © David L. Hughes

All rights reserved. No part of this work may be reproduced or stored in an information retrieval system (other than for purposes of review) without prior written permission by the copyright holder.

A catalogue record of this book is available from the British Library

First Edition: February 2019

ISBN: 978-1-84375-625-5

This is a work of fiction. Names, characters, places and incidents are the product of the author's imagination or are used fictitiously, and any resemblance to any actual persons, living or dead, events, or locales is entirely coincidental.

To order additional copies of this book please visit:
http://www.prestige-press.com/shirleyhughes

Published by: Prestige Press
Email: info@prestige-press.com
Web: http://www.prestige-press.com

Other Books by the author:

Persona
In Depth Of Soul
The Choices of Being
The Grass Isn't Always Greener
Rose Tinted Glasses
Leah's Journey
The Pink Flamingo Fellowship
Bilé
Academia
Pathway To The Unconscious
Sartre – In Focus
Mooloo
The Symbolic Mask
Ghostopia
Recognising The Soul

Transformation

by

Dr. Shirley Hughes

Prestige Press

Contents

	Note	9
	Introduction	11
1	Existentialism	13
2	The Existentialist	16
3	Freedom	21
4	The Price of Freedom	23
5	Freedom as Autonomy	26
6	Between Ourselves	29
7	Absurdity and Tragedy	32
8	Powerlessness	35
9	Depression	37
10	An Existentialist Film	43
11	Film Noir	46
12	Finding Truth	49
13	Goodwill Hunting	51
14	The Free Market Existentialist	55
15	Defining Ourselves	58
16	An Existentialist View	65
17	Affinity with the Arts	68
18	Performance Philosophy	70
19	Philosophy and Music	72
20	Existentialism as Punk	74
21	Relevant Existentialist	78
22	Existentialist Ethics	80
23	Existentialist Hero	82
24	Affirmative Response	85
25	Selfhood	88
26	Other People and Identity	90
27	Absurd Coping Strategies	93
28	Subject to Critcism	95
29	Autonomy	98
30	Two Ways	101
	In Conclusion	103

Note

In the throes of writing this book I am excited. I am standing on the shoulders of giants but my little ego would like to get some credit and some notoriety. I am excited because my ideas have relevance to what people are talking about, reading and studying today. The real attention for me is created by my feeling as a writer. I love to write and I get a kick out of doing so. I especially enjoy luxuriating in a project which obliges my mind to become engrossed.

The subject and scope of this current work demands all of my attention, knowledge and recollections. I also get to employ my full powers of craftsmanship which is another pleasure for me. This experience is an opportunity for me to find philosophical, consolation in one of the great philosophical questions of transformation and freedom.

Introduction

Welcome to Existentialism. It is one of the most important and fascinating philosophical movements of modern times. Its popularity never dies because its concerns are not merely of interest to scholars. It grapples with some of the biggest questions we all face in our lives. Questions of meaning, of freedom, of responsibility, of personal identity and authenticity, of religious belief, of morality and of the apparent absurdity of life. These questions also of course run through much of culture including art, music, theatre, cinema and literature. So it isn't surprising that people use Existentialist ideas to understand works of art or that some of the key philosophers of Existentialism are novelists and playwrights as well.

So what is this philosophy? What are its central assumptions and claims? It starts with the assumption that we are thrown into a universe that doesn't care about us and that we have no predetermined purpose to being here and no predetermined essence of who we are. So our existence comes first and who we are then becomes, through our freely chosen actions which are totally up to us. It is a very rich philosophy. If you think that philosophy should have the potential to change the way people live then Existentialism is one school of thought that you really have to study. This philosophy has its demons to fight having always put an emphasis on a commitment to truth and we philosophers have been quick to identify the obstacles that stand in the way of honouring this obligation.

Chapter 1

Existentialism

Existentialism is a philosophical movement that exercised an influence on many of the arts as well as on philosophy and psychology. Existentialists are diverse in their beliefs and what all existentialists have in common is a belief that for beings existence precedes essence meaning that there is no pre-existing blueprint for humanity, no human nature to which we must conform. We choose what we become. There is no God in whose mind our essence lies. We must first, and through our actions, make of ourselves what we will. In our choices we determine what sort of being each of us is. We are completely free to determine what we want to become but at the same time this freedom carries with it an inescapable burden.

A human being has no predetermined function and no divine artisan as maker in whose mind our essence could have been determined. The emphasis on human freedom to choose what we are and what we become is characteristic of all Existential thinkers. Existentialism is a form of humanism which is a term that has many related meanings. In one sense it simply applies to any theory that puts human beings at the centre of things. It has the positive connotations of being human. It is also a term for secular movements and those who reject the idea that there is a God who is the source of morality. It also emphasizes the dignity of humanity. The centrality of human choice to the creation of all values. It is another way of saying that human beings create what they are responsible for, what and whom we are and what we value. We also want to identify that human beings create morality. We also want to identify Existentialism as a humanism in order to identify the human psyche and human potential.

We assert that someone genuinely chooses to be free and therefore cannot not wish freedom for others assuming that logically what we want for ourselves we must want for other people. What we choose to do is always what we believe to be the better course of action but nothing can be better for us unless it is better for everyone. The image we create when making choices must hold for everyone.

Events and circumstances can prevent the realization of our goals but just because things may not turn out the way we hope does not warrant that we should abandon ourselves to inaction. Human beings are fundamentally free, that is the core of what we are. The position of making choices is one of anguish. We are not just free but condemned to be free. Human beings are free. This freedom can be an enormous burden and responsibility which we do not always wish to acknowledge. So we deceive ourselves pretending that, like mere physical objects we are wholly predetermined to be what we are and to believe the way we do when we deceive ourselves like this we are guilty of bad faith i.e. deceiving ourselves about the reality of situations. The Existentialist place human freedom at the centre of their philosophy. That we are free is not just a given but the fundamental truth about human beings.

For human beings existence precedes essence. Human beings differ from mere objects in that for humans existence does proceed essence. We exist but not for any particular purpose. Nor do we possess an intrinsic nature that determines how we will behave in the way that hearts do. What purpose we have and how we act must be freely chosen by us. This responsibility to choose is unavoidable. We are at every moment able to break free from old habits and the roles society has handed us. We are able right now to choose different values, to find new goals to forge ourselves anew.

Of course we don't choose the particular circumstances into

Transformation

which we are born. These circumstances will inevitably restrict what we are able to do. Nevertheless we are free to choose how we respond to these circumstances. We can choose to acquiesce or disobey and face the consequences. The fact that we have the freedom at each moment to break free from all our old habits and choices and forge ourselves anew is something of which we are all aware at some level but it is also something we can find hard to bear. We make our choices in anguish, abandonment and despair which is why we fall into bad faith and why we end up deceiving ourselves about this radical freedom. We are confronted with this unavoidable responsibility to choose and expose the deceptions we perpetrate on ourselves in order to try to avoid it. We are free but how can we be so sure? If human beings are physical objects then they are governed by the same laws of nature that governs all physical objects so then they are surely not free. They merely think they are. Belief in our freedom appears to be based on a subjective awareness. It feels to us from the inside as if we are free but this feeling may be deceptive. We philosophers have certainly struggled to explain how it is possible for human beings to be both free and also subject to the same laws of nature and other physical objects.

Chapter 2

The Existentialist

How to become authentically Existentialist.

It took a century of thought before Existentialism came to fruition as a popular movement and was almost a craze in post-war France in the forties and fifties. This was the time of its greatest influence not only on philosophy but on all art and extended far beyond France. All philosophers in the Existentialist camp shared the same mission to make us recognise that human beings are free and free to choose not only what to do when faced with moral choices but what to value and how to live. They wanted the facts about human freedom to be not merely accepted but absorbed by each person individually so that when they have absorbed then their whole view of life will be different.

Existentialism as a cultural movement belongs in the past but as a philosophy with this utterly practical mission it can be as liberating to us now as it was in those war torn times in Western Europe. When readers of the Parisian newspapers such as Le Monde began to take notice of Existentialism it published an article to tell them what it meant but did admit that Existentialism like faith cannot be explained. It can only be lived.

Why is it like faith? Because to base one's conduct on a belief that one is free to choose is an act of faith for there is no way of knowing for sure whether it is true or false. What makes Existentialism hard to explain is that it claims that to seek a code for behaviour anywhere outside of ourselves makes it futile because it claims that

Transformation

no objective moral code exists independently of humanity. Each individual has to create his or her own value by living and affirming it and must do so in the way that satisfies a single governing norm of authenticity in perhaps over simplistic terms through always being one's self.

Existentialism is obsessed with how individuals choose to live their lives. Our choices are demonstrated by our acts and always concern matters within our power. To choose then, involves deliberating about things that are in our control and attainable by our action. Then by whatever actions we choose to take we define and create the selves that we gradually become.

For example, we become 'just' by performing just acts and similarly as regards other virtues. This is not meant as a moral point no should or ought is implied but a fact about the nature of the world and of human choices that my choices of good or evil will determine my character and make me the kind of human being that I turn out to be.

Existentialism obviously rests on some pretty bold ontological assumptions then, claims about what society and how it exists. The first is that values are not part of the fabric of the world, in the sense of existing independently of us. To live your life as if your values were somehow given from outside, as though to adopt the attitude of an upright, conventional person whose duties all seem to be laid out for them, would amount to a refusal to face up to your freedom. In that case you wrongly think that you can escape your freedom by taking refuge in a fixed role or essence. Even when people do adopt ready-made values in this way they still choose to do so, albeit it in a way that has failed to live up to the value of authenticity because it doesn't recognise their inalienable freedom.

My attitude is authentic when I engage in my project as my own. My attitude would not be authentic if keeping my promises for instance is something I do because of that's what society expects of me. My way of behaving is authentic if and only if my action is a reflection of my choice, that is, when I commit myself to behave in that sort of way because that is what I expect of myself whether or not it is socially sanctioned.

Existentialism makes every individual responsible for deciding for themselves how to evaluate their choices. It is in the nature of values that they make demands on us. To value a certain way of acting more highly than any alternative is to choose that particular way as a goal to set up an ideal to be aimed at. Although the values you adopt are indeed your values they do not merely express your private feelings about what is right or wrong then. For the concept of choice entails the idea of whatever is chosen is the right thing to do and a right means right for everyone that is when a man chooses for himself he chooses for mankind, meaning for every action we choose provides an example for the rest of humanity. If I choose a particular good for myself such as freedom I am therefore committed to choosing freedom for everyone.

Freedom

Chapter 3

Freedom

Existentialisms most basic premise is that human beings have no pre-existing or set nature or character. We are not essentially anything except that we are essentially free. We become self-created beings by virtue of our actions and our relations with other people. Hence the Existentialist slogan existence precedes essence. That each one of us has absolute freedom of choice is an Existentialist article of faith. To the Existentialist it is a truth so self-evident that it never needs to be proved or even argued for and who needs a theoretical proof of something indispensable to the practical business of living?

To the Existentialist my freedom is my essence and my salvation. I cannot lose it without ceasing to be. So every honest person must recognise my freedom. Obviously no one chooses entirely what he or she becomes or is. Each of us has a set of given natural and social properties that influence the kind of person we become. To these features the collective name is facticity. One's facticity comprises all of those properties such as sex, weight, height and skin colour, social facts such as race, class, nationality, psychological properties, such as extant web of beliefs, desires, character traits and historical facts such as a family background, schooling and so forth. All these properties another person could discover and investigate.

Our own facticity hardly ever occupies our own minds in this third person kind of way even though it does weigh on us and colour our moods and approach to life. However, when we do step back and take a third person objective view of our facticity then these given facts about us may strike us as precisely what does define who we are. But for an existentialist, to think this would be a radical mistake, not because our factual properties are misleading but the person each one of us is cannot be defined in third person terms. No objective account of my properties could ever describe my subjective experience of what it's like to be me, the person who has them.

So someone observing me can make out my skin colour, class or ethnicity but the moment he attempts to identify me in terms of these properties he encounters a paradox, since the kind of being I am is defined among other things by the attitude I adopt towards my own facticity by how I choose to interpret it and that is not fixed by the facts. Who I am depends among other things on what I make of my facticity, by how I try to go beyond or transcend it. In other words whatever my facticity and no matter how fixed it might be, it does not curtail my freedom. I am still free to decide what values to ascribe to my facticity and what stance to take towards it.

To become the person you choose to be despite the burden of your facticity is the only authentic way to live your life, whereas to live it as though you were at the mercy of your facticity to pretend that it has robbed you of your freedom is inauthenticity. It would be to lose both one's autonomy and one's integrity and in this way give in to determinism.

Chapter 4

The Price of Freedom

It would be hard to feel otherwise about freedom and choice if you had lived in occupied France between 1940 and 1945 when Existentialism came of age as the official philosophy of the resistance movement. In those and even after, post 1945, reconstructing it exerted a powerful appeal that was as much emotional as intellectual. If man is nothing but that which he makes of himself, then no one is bound by fate or by forces outside that control. By uniting with like-minded people, the individual can change authority, even tyrannical power and change things. They could choose to oppose the Nazis or to create a more just society that had existed before the war. Only by exercising their personal freedom could people regain civil liberties. But there is a price to be paid for freedom to whatever you choose at every juncture. No one can decide on your behalf.

The choice of action is always yours and yours alone and no one can avoid the personal responsibility for judging what the morally right thing to do is. You thus suffer the potential anguish of having to endure an endless series of choices in the knowledge that only you can decide that you may invade and evaluate anything as you please, and that you have no character to guide your choices other than the one you're forming for yourself. Not everyone can cope with the burden of an Existentialist approach to shaping their lives and characters. Some may triy to flee the tyranny of choice by hiding from themselves the truth that we are all condemned to be free which means not free to cease being free. All our acts inevitably presuppose choice and so we are still choosing even when we think we are not, even when we have deliberately chosen not to choose.

When France was overrun and occupied by the German army in 1940 every French man and woman was forced to think about their values and decide whether to resist and struggle to free their country or to resign themselves to Nazi domination. They had to choose and it was a time when they faced their freedom in great anguish. Some were unable to bear the thought of their freedom and in order to escape the pressure adopted the cover of a bad faith perhaps the most important concept of this philosophy. Someone is in bad faith when in order to protect himself from the anxiety of having to choose he pretends to himself that he is not so free as he actually is. It is a specific kind of self-deception, a core betrayal of one's self. A common type of bad faith is the denial of one's freedom in the form of an excuse, typically beginning with "I couldn't help it"….. We hear this in the excuse made by those Nazi soldiers who insisted "I could not do otherwise. I was just doing my duty".

One can always do otherwise. One can quit or run away or even choose to be shot. The cost might be enormous, even one's life, but it is never the case of cannot but always of will not. They choose to obey orders. It was not determined by their nature. Existentialism doesn't allow excuses. There is never a legitimate reason for saying once freedom is denied. No matter how repressed or oppressed we may be by our situation or circumstances we know we can always imagine alternatives and act on them two, if we are brave enough. The only way to stay in good faith is honesty to continually own up and respond to being free to choose and accountable for whatever you decide to do. Thinking and living I detect in the language the characteristic missionary tone of Existentialism which implores us all to experience our freedom to choose and to practice it.

Existentialism is a coherent theory rooted in an idealist, that is a consciousness based metaphysics but it is not enough to merely understand it intellectually that way. To grasp it properly one has to engage with it as a practical and committed philosophy in other words to commit to being an existentialist. Then you would see yourself as free and autonomous in the way you did not recognise before and by doing so acquire the power to transcend your facticity.

Facticity and transcendence are grand concepts of Existentialism. Our Facticity defines our situation and who we are up to this point in our lives. Transcendence opens up the world of possibilities, what we now can go on to make of that situation and of ourselves given who or what we have become so far. Existentialism is absolutely not academic. It is the antithesis of the purely analytical approach to philosophy, the prime purpose of which seems to be to deliver mental hygiene. The whole point of Existentialism is to practice its liberating ideas, to apply them to becoming the person one chooses to be. That we can be the authors of our own lives and characters strike me as a very appealing thought. It means that life in a sense can be in itself become the stuff of art, something to be shaped according to one's own vision of one's self.

Chapter 5

Freedom as Autonomy

Freedom is an emotive concept evoking thoughts and feelings relating to rights, entitlements, possibilities, and limitations. It is also a complex concept fraught with ambiguity. This complex issue of freedom and particularly of moral freedom is inevitably linked to issues of personal responsibility and accountability. In our everyday lives do we freely choose our actions and attitudes or is our behaviour determined by factors outside our control and what do we mean by freedom?

Sometimes freedom is understood negatively as freedom from hunger, poverty, illness or threat. This interpretation of freedom is intrinsically linked with a desire for security and safety, wellbeing and control. We see plenty of situations in the political, social and personal realms where the desire for the freedom from any threat to that security is translated into a call for the diminishment of the freedom of others. Freedom from our fears comes at a price. We also desire freedom to do certain things specifically to think to choose and to act according to our own point of view, our conscience or moral code. This is the basis of personal autonomy where the individual is the author of his or her own rules values and desires even if these have been appropriated from external sources consciously or unconsciously.

Is such personal autonomy a universal right or is the idea of it conditional on social, cultural, legal and institutional precepts and moral codes? We have all experienced situations where it doesn't seem safe to exercise our personal autonomy through self-

Transformation

expression or dissent. These are situations of vulnerability resulting from perceived or a real imbalance of power. There can sometimes be a failure to recognise autonomy by failing to treat people with proper human dignity. Sometimes human rights do not extend to all humans. There is an underlying and unwavering belief in the freedom of the individual to decide for ourselves. The intrinsic foundation of the concept of freedom is personal responsibility for one's actions.

The other side of autonomy is the impossibility of excuses or the abdication of personal responsibility. Even in the relatively normal situations of our lives do we freely choose who we are and what we do? Choosing a philosophy of freedom….. Freedom of choice is the chief characteristic of the human condition. As existentialists we reject any idea that we, our choices or our actions are completely determined by forces outside our control, our biology, biography, personality or situation could not be called upon either as excuses for or explanation of our actions. Man is free man is freedom. We reject the unconscious because on some level we even exercise a choice regarding which material we repress from conscious awareness so the unconscious cannot be called upon as an excuse for our behaviour or actions.

We also reject any notion of a pre-given meaning of life either for individual life or for life in general that is man makes himself. He isn't ready-made at the start. There are no pre-established essentials regarding human nature. Each person creates his or her own essence of meaning in an ongoing process of deciding and acting. Before we became alive, life is nothing. It is up to us to give it meaning and value if nothing else, but the meaning that we choose. We must make these choices at every moment and in every situation because there is no pre-meaning of value which may be applied to any particular situation. Each situation is encountered freely, without recourse to previously established judgments or dictates and it demands a choice on our part. Man is always the same. It is the situation that confronts him varies. What does exist is a universal human condition which is we must make choices. We are condemned to be free because once thrown into the world we are responsible for everything we do. We do not have the freedom to refuse our freedom. What is not possible is not to choose. We can always choose but ought to know that if we do not choose we are still choosing. If we accept this that everything in our lives is the result of our own choices and decisions. Is freedom then the question of choosing one's attitude to circumstances which are outside our control? We have the freedom to choose our attitude in all situations, to choose one's way. We dismiss the notions of a preordained meaning, purpose in life or of a predetermined essence or nature to individuals.

Man is not fully conditioned and determined but rather determines himself whether he gives into conditions or stands up to them. Man is ultimately self-determining. He always decides what his erxistence will be and what he will become in the next moment. Therefore, regardless of our material or physical conditions our attitude and our corresponding behaviour is always a free choice. We are not determined by biology, circumstances or personality then and we are not helpless victims. We are self-determined and with have the power to create our own destiny. The absence of a predetermined or preordained meaning or purpose does not preclude the individual's freedom and responsibility to create his or her own meaning, values and purpose. In fact it insists on the necessity of doing so. Existentialist philosophy is demanding and ethical and the focus on individual freedom and responsibility is intrinsically related to subjective interpretation of choice.

Chapter 6

Between Ourselves

Existentialism is often criticised for its apparent nihilism, negativity and bleakness. Its insistence on the essential meaninglessness of life, the absurdity of the human condition, is sometimes interpreted as defeatist and hopeless. Existentialists argue however that the absence of a preordained meaning or purpose does not preclude the individual's freedom and responsibility to create his or her own meaning, values and purpose. In fact it insists on the necessity of doing so.

This philosophy is demanding and ethical. The focus on individual freedom and responsibility is intrinsically related to subjective interpretation and choice. However it also demands a simultaneous awareness of other's freedom and responsibility. Each individual lives in the world inhabited by others and their choices and actions inevitably have an impact on others in particular as they contribute to the image another may have on themselves at any particular moment. Because one's self is in the world one's acts are never simply one's own. This leads us to describe the focus of this Existentialism as inter subjectivity. If we accept the essentialist premise of my own freedom and responsibility by virtue of the fact that we are human beings then we logically must also extend this conviction to all human beings.

Our freedom to choose, to make decisions and to act in accordance with our own judgment and our values implies a similar inescapable freedom for others. The dignity of the human being entails the freedom to think and to act for oneself, while it simultaneously ascribes responsibility to each individual. We want freedom for ourselves, for freedom sake and in every particular circumstance and in wanting freedom we discover that it depends on the freedom of others. Therefore Existentialism is opposed to tyranny of any kind, political, economic, moral or personal. There is no room for domination or authoritarianism, by the law giver, the expert or that do-gooder. The inner subjective nature of the self-explores the concept of the 'look'. Whereby the individual sense of self is affected to a considerable extent by the knowledge of being perceived by others, an example of this phenomenon concerns the feeling of shame.

Someone may participate in a certain behaviour when caught in the act or seen by another then a feeling of shame ensues. The other is the indispensable mediator between myself and me as I am ashamed of myself as I appear to another. It is evident from this that self-knowledge involves a mediation between self and others. In order to get any truth about ourselves we must have contact with others. In order to get any truth the awareness of another perception may also prompt an inauthentic performance on the part of the individual in an attempt to convey a more favourable impression.

In the analysis of human motivation and behaviour looking behind the physical and verbal expression of some familiar emotions like compassion, sympathy, outrage and grief suggests that behind the outward show of expected responses lurks an ever present concern with the audience. Ultimately not even the deepest pain can keep the actor from thinking of the impression of his part and the overall theatrical affect so the perception may elucidate self-knowledge and self-understanding but it may also provide the motivation for subterfuge and pretence where one may distort one's sense of identity to fit the image thought to be held by other people. This would be considered by existentialists as an example of bad faith which is the attitude where one has self-deceptively relinquished the possibility of self-creation and self-expression in order to try and be something fixed and dependent on other people's perception of what you are or should be.

There are aspects of every life which remains hidden and

Transformation

incommunicable and an unease at the thought of being defined through others' perceptions can actively be a significant one. What spoils relations among people is that each keeps something hidden from the other, things that refuse to be said and which can only be said to oneself and which resists being said to another. As with other people there is a depth of distress within that does not allow itself to be said. Is the conception of human freedom compatible with our personal experience or is it extreme in its demands and its responsibilities? Does it remain just a theory or can we actually live up to it?

Chapter 7

Absurdity and Tragedy

Absurdity is another important theme in Existentialism. Absurdity in the Existentialist sense is the contrast between human values, hopes and projects and a universe which seems mockingly indifferent to them. There is a belief on the strength of the absurd. Existentialists juxtapose understanding and the absurd. It is said "Faith hopes for this life also, but not well, by virtue of the absurd not by virtue of the human understanding. To see God or to see a miracle is by virtue of the absurd, for understanding must step aside". In this way absurdity is used to express the limits of reason and especially of pure reason but in agreement with atheist existentialists who often speak of the importance of human reason but in disagreement when spoken of a God reached by 'the leap of faith'.

Some treat absurdity not just as something opposed to reason but as a central quality of human existence. Some protagonists do not conform to the social system they are born into because they see life as absurd that they are condemned because they do not play the game. Some use the epidemic to reveal the absurdity of the human condition. Those caught in the plague have to deal with their own individual Existential issues but eventually find themselves in solidarity with the infected. Many religiously inclined people have argued that some existentialists thoughts on meaninglessness and absurdity lead people to immorality, nihilism and despair so doesn't the philosophy that insists upon the absurdity of the world run the risk of driving people to despair?

Accepting the absurdity of everything around us is one step in a necessary experience. It should not become a dead end. It arouses a revolt that can become fruitful. So a recognition of absurdity can create an impetus for positive social change. Tragedy and absurdity are given, partially understood by the intellect and deeply felt at the level of the emotions. In religious Existentialism there is always something to which tragedy and absurdity point but they are not a means to an end. To take tragedy and absurdity seriously and to their logical conclusion then it is easy to see how this can give us a radical and life affirming philosophy for the 21st century. If we accept these themes of the Existentialist literature with seriousness and if all responsibility is on us, then since themes of Existentialism cannot be answered, remedied or overcome they should be embraced and used as a way of affirming one's individuality and as an impetus towards living authentically.

What follows from this is a philosophy of action and if there were ever a time when an Existential philosophy of human responsibility were needed it would surely be now. Instead of examining and evaluating the ways in which we live our lives we are offered quick and easy answers but we don't need answers as much as we need honesty.

Religious Existentialism can help modern society by providing people with a philosophy that accepts the tragedy and absurdity of existence while promoting responsibility and authentic living. It can help people move past resignation promoting responsibility which provides an ethic that honours individual projects and social responsibility and encourages the sympathy and empathy that arises through communication. Absurdity first and foremost is a function of consciousness. Only consciousness can offer the awareness of the absurd thereby creating absurdity and once experienced it can never be forgotten.

The struggle against the absurd is consciousness's ultimate battle. Death is the extreme symbol of the absurd since death represents both the cessation of consciousness and an unknowable phenomenon. Therefore tragic knowledge or absolute and radical tragedy compares to notions of meaningless or absurdity. Carrying radical tragedy to its logical conclusion is to say that every existing thing is born without reason, prolongs itself out of weakness and dies by chance. Taking tragedy and absurdity seriously requires a belief in the non-existence of God's and an afterlife. Tragedy and absurdity fit well in a Godless world. Given a religious spin they'd lose of their strengths and fecundity. Tragedy is absolute and absurdity is complete.

Chapter 8

Powerlessness

Many Existential philosophers have described, sometimes in vivid detail what it is like to feel powerless. Social and political forces external to us can take away our freedoms and impugn us with guilt creating a sense of powerlessness. Psychological forces internal to us can do the same thing. The internal forces are especially frightening because they occur inside us and yet can feel beyond our control. They can inculcate feelings of isolation, fear and dread, along with a sense of being trapped in our own personality. A good way to explore the feeling of powerlessness is through the work of those who have examined it in great detail. The best examples of this are several Existential philosophers and philosophical novelists who are well acquainted with the forces both external and internal and think we ought to harness the power of our desires and affirms us by willing to live with dangerous confidence.

Others depicted the individual as powerless, weak and passive, a victim of forces beyond our control. The greatness of philosophy is that it encourages, uplifts, empowers and revitalises. It tells the individual to conquer fear and self-pity by affirming our unique power in the world. It tells us that the greatness and fruitfulness and the greatness of enjoyment of existence is to live dangerously. Live at war with our peers and ourselves. Be lovers of knowledge. It thinks of us as actively engaged in the world and not as a passive product of circumstances. Some show how powerless humans are in the face of forces beyond their control. Some present stories, allegories of where the theme of powerless is central. The never ending struggle illustrates the never ending torment of those who feel powerless, a whole life struggling to move the boulder so to speak and imagining the unhappiness this way of life is.

Although some people try but never know what their purpose is and never come to terms with it ends in a constant war against the invisible. They are subject to the whims of powers outside of their control. Depression sets in when they never accomplish any meaningful changes in what they see as the lot they were given. Wisdom involves knowing when we can change things and when we cannot. We cannot change, courage changes the things we can and wisdom to know the difference. There is a famous 'serenity prayer' which says "grant us to accept the things we cannot change". It contains a kernel of truth. Whether or not we ought to orientate ourselves in a manner similar to the Existential philosophers is a different matter and question. The fact is we all ought to act as if we can change things, conquer fears and affirm our lives. The responsibility of our lives, our projects and our personalities is on ourselves since we are the authors of our own life stories.

Chapter 9

Depression

Existentialism can be a treatment for depression. Colloquially the word depression is often used for listlessness, extreme sadness or a profound sense of loss. It is no wonder that so many people with a diagnosis of depression struggle to be taken seriously. To the unaffected the problem sounds akin to a diagnosis of sadness but sadness in fact is not the only or even the main complaint a clinical diagnosis requires. It needs at least five symptoms and only one of those refers to a depressed mood.

Depression is exhausting. Feelings of listlessness and fatigue saturate life and everyday tasks become laborious as though walking through and wading through tar. Things which previously gave joy rest become encumbering and socialising is a chore. Shadows creep across the walls of the mind. Depression is not the same as sadness. Sadness is transient, depression is pervasive. It is difficult as depression is like schizophrenia in the sense that both disorders are those of perception. It is hard to accept the extent to which our emotions warp our reality.

In a depressed state the veil of happiness has been taken away. The depressive comes to believe the worthlessness, either of their own or the world's and this belief appears infallible despite evidence to the contrary. The nature of the link between perception and reality is one of the oldest philosophical debates. The debate is also one without resolution. Even if what we perceive as reality may not be reality we have no choice but to continue behaving as if it were. Yet from a neuro psychological perspective the possibility that our own grasp of reality is limited or even corrupted, is almost a certainty. Our brains provide our only window to the world and like any other organ they are fallible and prone to malfunction.

Our brains are capable of creating false memories. We mistake dreams for reality and we fall for optical illusion. Hallucinogenic drugs symptomatically distant perception. Existentialist philosophers discuss the nature of experience from the perspective of meaning and morality, arguing that the world is intrinsically meaningless. The realization can be the source of anguish and anxiety. If life is intrinsically meaningless then why live it? The Existentialist solution to this nihilistic dread is autonomy. Within Existentialist philosophy the onus is on us to define our values and to act in a way that is consistent with it so shaping of ourselves. We are thus to reject the social roles and assumptions thrust upon us by others and discover our authentic selves. The self only becomes authentic when it is consciously constructed until we do that we are merely a patchwork of our genes, culture, upbringing and experiences.

Discovering the authentic self also means making decisions about the version of reality we choose to accept. By definition this process is subjective and it can be applied to help treat clinical depression. People who have overcome depression talk about it as a restorative process, a disintegration and subsequent rebuilding of the self. Severe depression can be crippling but these phases will often naturally give away to periods of remission. In these states a beneficial re-evaluation of perception can be sought. This can involve questioning deeply ingrained thought patterns reassessing personal values and evaluating one's personal development. Because the immediate causes of depression will be different for every person afflicted with it, overcoming it also requires introspection.

The value of agency comes into play here. Often depression can arise seemingly out of nowhere causing significant confusion and distress to a person. Other times depression follows a catalyst, the loss of a loved one or a significant personal failure. The negative aspects of life which can serve to exacerbate depression can sometimes be removed e.g. a toxic relationship or under fulfilling job. However we may accept that our agency is limited. We will

Transformation

also be tethered to our basic biological needs and the construction of our values. This is perhaps the only sphere in which our own agency is absolute. The pursuit of authenticity allows us to set our own parameters here. Ultimately depression is the consequence of genetic predisposition here. Also chemical dysfunction and on many cases a catalyst. Fallacies in perception and interpretation perpetuates depression and we have the agency to alter these.

People with depression are often reluctant to try drug therapies because they warp their reality and sacrifice their authenticity. In the medicated mind is it artificial or does medication restore normality to a mind that is deficient? Am I still myself if every day I take medication which changes how I feel and think? Seeking treatment can also feel like lying to yourself if one is unworthy of life then one is certainly unworthy of treatment. Viewing the world through depression can give the impression of finally seeing things for what they are.

Through Existentialist thinking however it is possible to break down those sorts of assumptions. If no values are objectively true then the depressed mind can be revaluated. Through Existentialist eyes we can see that refusing treatment on the basis of medications effects on one's objective reality on the authentic a medicated self is invalid. Depression can often be devastating but in cases where revaluation can lead to the creation of an authentic self, the person can be transformed.

Existentialist Films

Chapter 10

Revolutionary Road

This film is an Existentialist film directed by Sam Mendes and is an inspired screenplay. Viewers follow a couple from setback to setback as the unhappy couple readjust and compromise their dreams of living interesting advent-garde lives as they conform to the standard roles of husband and wife. They always imagined themselves different from others but they are like all the other husbands and wives in the falsely idyllic suburbs in which they live but this illusion fades before their eyes as the film moves forward. Neither of them asked for this kind of life and yet both of them are living and hating each other for it in their own small ways and denying one of the most important tenants of Existentialism, taking responsibility. Their fights lead to affairs and their affairs lead to fights. Their relationship is built on needs not met and there seems no way out but is there a way out after all?

The main actress is the star. Without her inner torment there would be no Existential conflict. She decides to take control to meet the enemy head on. Existentialism being concerned with the freedom of choice and what one does with it tells us that we are not only fundamentally free to choose but obliged to make authentic choices. To choose authentically means we are individually responsible to undertake the challenge of continually creating ourselves. This Existentialist responsibility is often misunderstood as dark, moody and just plain depressing when in fact it is a call to action, described as the sternness of our optimism.

After years of denial she finally sees her responsibility for her own life and understands that she and her husband have not been true to themselves. She comes up with a plan to go to Paris where her husband was stationed during his time in the military and is the only place he ever talked of returning to. She decides they must move there for good. She sees this as a chance to change their course and set things right. She discovers she can get a good job and make good money overseas and her husband can finally take time off and discover what he really wants to do with his life, i.e. reading, studying, taking long walks and thinking for the first time in his life he will have time to find out what it is he wants to do, and when he finds it he will have the time and freedom to start doing it.

Paris is their Shangri-La and if she can convince him they'll leave the wretched suburbs behind for ever. However there is a problem and she doesn't see the obvious. The plan instantly frightens her husband for all his brave talk he seems to fit the role of coward. He says he despises his job but appears to find comfort in it. He is disenchanted with the dull routine of his days but discovers relief in the tedium. This is the stuff of Existentialism and Existentialism is best served on a literary plate. Many seminal works of Existentialism translate well into films. The internal monologue, the ruminating self-evaluation and Angst the subtle things that make living in the world absurd have always produced greater literature but not always riveting cinema. A colleague asks, "what is the real reason? You've got cold feet, you decide you like it here after all, you figure is more comfortable here in the old hopeless emptiness?"

His colleague is the only one who has the courage to speak the truth. It is an Existential wake up call. She has missed her window of opportunity and her husband is responsible for the cold calculated dismantling of their dream. In the end they suffer not from what they believe to be the trap society has set for them but for refusing to act. Revolutionary Reassessment. The film is highly recommended. We went off and get the chance to see good Existentialism on the big screen. There is no tosh in this tale of self-inflicted wounds. The people must take responsibility for themselves whatever the situation. We are alone without excuses and that is what's meant when it is said that we are condemned to

Transformation

be free. This film is about truth of human experience. This film is a classic story of disappointment and loss. It expertly pulls apart the social order and how we all compromise ourselves to death behind a veneer of cosy acquiescence.

It's a whole new disturbing ball game. She just needs everyone to shut up so she can put it all in perspective. In the final scene as it fades to black in one of the few humorous moments in an otherwise uncompromising relentless talk of Existential angst she finally gets her wish. It demonstrates an epic game changer an epic collapse that forces us to take a long hard look at who we are and what it means to be alive in a world that has turned against us a moment that makes us realise and reassess a lifelong dream and decide whether it's time to give up on it for good and we just need a little time and space to think it through put it all in perspective rearrange the psyche to cope with the death of our dreams. Is the film Existentialist or just depressing?

Chapter 11

Film Noir

Film Noir represents a dark night of the soul in cinema. These films are made in the 1940's and 1950's referred to as Film Noir convey dark feelings of disillusionment, pessimism and cynicism. Recurring characteristics of these films are that the whole society portrayed seems corrupt, that protagonist is a cunning exploiter and fatalism rules as plans go away, and this is how crime is presented. The protagonist is more antihero, a femme fatale lures the protagonist into crime.

The expressionistic use of black and white photography which gives Film Noir its name emphasises the bleak reality of urban life and the disillusionment it brings. Film Noir has been written about extensively highlighting philosophical aspects of the genre or what to aesthetics issues from ontology one of a wide range of issues. Does its fatalism equate with tragedy, to the meaning of life in its cynicism founded on a moral crisis such as Existential angst and more? The phenomenon of Film Noir invites a sociological speculation. On social context is emphasized the trauma of war, the difficulties encountered post-war when survivors tried to resume a normal life. Film Noir gave expression to those kinds of social problems. Such speculations are tempting but they are methodological dubious since they make broad sociological comments usually with little empirical data to support them.

For the most part contributors to this anthology avoid such speculation and concentrate on the film's rather than on the society in which they were made. They examine the fatalistic outlook

Transformation

found in many classic noir films and compares it to the concept of absurdity in Existentialism. In these films the protagonist seems doomed, plans do not work out, human relationships are flawed and unreliable and society seems biased in favour of others. That combination of fatalism and alienation has some kinship with Existentialism.

The Existentialist is alienated because of the refusal to accept as given the moral codes of others. According to Existential philosophers anyone who denies their freedom by following a perceived moral code is guilty of bad faith. This freedom however brings absurdity in its wake because the world is indifferent to the hopes of humanity. Such Existentialist defiance of the absurd world is expressed in the dark with which is a feature of Film Noir. However we conclude that Film Noir and Existentialism are fundamentally different in their attitude to human freedom.

Both recognise that our freedom is bounded by physical limits but Existentialism emphasises the capacities that humans have – the scope of our freedom – whereas Film Noir sees only contingency failure and fate. A similar analysis of the fatalism in Film Noir lead some to conclude that despite the combination of flawed heroes and pessimistic outcomes the narratives do not attain the status of tragedy. In some totalitarian terms Film Noir is no drama and stories morally incoherent. They provide glimpses of personal integrity but no clashes of principle which test the moral fibre of the protagonist thus falling short of tragedy. Some of this is quite persuasive but some were less so. The pessimism of noir is one of its strengths because pessimism is more realistic than optimism. That assertion is contentious in itself leaving us wondering whether pessimism is realistic, distorted or both. Equally debatable was the identification of a lack of religious faith with meaninglessness, alienation or a lack of moral values, the world of Film Noir being largely God free.

Discussion of Film Noir is often too narrowly focused. The classics of Film Noir stirs the emotions, killings happen and we are morally implicated by our sympathy for the wrong doers. We feel more sympathy for the killers than for their victims. Ordinary moral reasoning seems to be undermined. It can be argued convincingly that morality ultimately rests on our emotions of sympathy and compassion. Those feelings provide the ought - the basic moral values from which all our complex moral reasonings are derived. It's assumed our sympathies would follow a conventional path and cherish our common humanity.

The challenge of Film Noir is to deny that assumption and depict a world where our sympathies take a different path that leaves us down darker alleyways. Perhaps that is part of the attraction. We enter a world where our moral bearings are lost and we allow ourselves to side with amoral people living in a world quite like our own but with all its ugly, unjust defects emphasized. We cannot tell how well we shall cope confronting murky situations with our moral complacency switched off but that uncertainty grips our conscience and our attention and carries us into the story.

Philosophy is the art of putting our thoughts in order but doing that requires us to scatter the pieces sometimes just to see how we again arrive at order from disorder. Film Noir performs such a function for our moral thinking and does so in a most engaging way. Delving into the film's and elucidating their philosophical depths is also challenging and engaging so prepare to be provoked.

Chapter 12

Finding Truth

There is a general tendency in the non-philosophical world to dismiss Existential philosophy as being purely theoretical with no connection to the types of problems that people are confronted with in their everyday lives but this is not necessarily true. Many philosophers struggle to find ways to improve people's lives by drawing attention to and making people think about fundamental aspects of life. Some sought to answer life's questions by turning back to ancient times to thinkers who are felt to be closer in mind and spirit. However Existential philosophers tried to challenge the common beliefs of our time to show that the only truth that is important is subjective truth. Only through a deep and honest analysis of oneself that anyone truly know what is or is not, what one's values and beliefs are and what one's truths.

Each individual can and should think for themselves and so find their own paths in life and their own value. This can be done by a close examination of one's thinking. The technique of helping people become aware of their own knowledge is known as maieutic. The thing is to find a truth which is a truth for you, to find the idea for which each of us is willing to live and die. What would it be in this respect if we were to discover a so called objective truth or if we worked our way through the philosophical systems and what use would it be in that respect to be able to work out a theory of the state which we ourselves did not inhabit but merely held up for others to see? What would it be to be able to propound and explain many separate facts if it has no deeper meaning for ourselves and our lives? We must first learn to know ourselves before knowing anything else. Only when we have inwardly understood ourselves and seen the way forward on our path does our lives acquire repose and meaning.

Each person is an embodiment of a way of seeing the world, a way of living their lives. It suggests that there are three main parts of life, the aesthetic, the ethical and the religious. The aesthete sees the world through an interesting but boring dichotomy. For him a life is made to live, to experience and there are no serious choices. Life is immediate for him. For the ethicist on the contrary, there are only serious choices. For him life is what you make of it. It is not enough to just live it. You must make concrete choices that will give shape to your existence to yourself. Life is responsibility, the religious on the other hand acknowledges that you cannot succeed in creating a perfect self, but through faith in God's forgiveness you can accept you're in perfect condition and live your life as yourself and this is the belief of the religious. However although these options look a lot like they represent ultimate solutions life possibilities are just that, possibilities. None of them represents an ultimate truth. They are merely choices that one can make in one's life. The Existential approach is relevant because of its focus on the individual.

Each one feels the need for purpose and this purpose can be gained only by our choices, our actions and the way we live our lives. No one can tell us who or what we are or what we should do. We must discover and decide that for ourselves in our inner most intimate place where we can make our true self come to light, then shine upon our own singular path. It is important for us to know ourselves, to discover what our values really are, our beliefs, our truths in order to live a more fulfilling life. It is important to know who we truly are so that nobody can manipulate us into doing what is contrary to our inner selves.

We do not present anyone with absolute objective truths but challenges each one to discover subjective truths for yourselves, to encourage independence. The phrase 'know yourself' means separate yourself from others. In the end what's Existential philosophy does is dare us to live by choosing how we live and by taking responsibility for our lives.

Chapter 13

Good Will Hunting

Good will hunting is a film worth giving an Existential analysis to. It is an encounter between a young working class prodigy and a burnt out middle aged therapist. It is a story of a relationship which deeply touches, upsets and inspires both men, to the extent that they both end up leaving behind the comfort of their old habits and houses and leave town.

The older man who was an Existentialist therapist whose thinking focused on the nature of perspective and on the nature of human encounters and this is a movie about what it takes from his perspective to be liberated from binding fears and take the dreadful first step that leads towards deeper awareness, more freedom and a higher level of responsibility. The opening of the movie depicts the young prodigy in a shabby bare house on the outskirts of the city sitting speed-reading a book surrounded by carelessly scattered books. He works as a janitor at the university, an average working class lifestyle in contrast with the brilliant intellect he possesses.

In a break from mopping floors he sketches the solution to an extremely difficult mathematical problem left on the university chalkboard. This prompts a professor of mathematics to seek him out. Meantime the young man is being held in custody for assaulting a policeman. Thanks to the professor's intervention he avoids a jail sentence only if he agrees to regularly see a therapist. After several failed attempts with various therapists he finally accepts authority of one who is originally from the same neighbourhood and social background as himself.

He stands up to the boy's arrogant attempts to disqualify him and eventually tames him into cooperation. It is difficult to assess the right session therapeutic intervention presented in the movie from a professional point of view. The session rather than therapy could be viewed as encounters in a special situation between two men with similar routes. The young prodigy is also to be seen as the therapist's own swansong his last case ever so intuitively feeling that the looming life change and Existential challenge that this encounter poses, he breaks all the rules of the art of therapy.

As a master of the art of therapy he plays his last game freestyle, sometimes even recklessly and dangerously. The treatment takes on the character of true horizontality and gains an Existential quality for both parties. Although it is not entirely clear which school the therapist follows we can safely say that this therapy bears many parts of the Existentialist humanistic treatment. Indeed the encounter between the two men serves as a beautiful illustration of the underlying premises of the Existentialist approach especially what can be called the I, thou relationship. From this perspective we can re-examine it as a sign of deepest respect by losing his presence, the therapist exposes himself to the patient and becomes extremely vulnerable. He is not only trying to teach the young man that there are certain limits he is also taking a risk. The young man could easily have used the fact of being attacked by the therapist against him. Instead he feels that he is being taken seriously by someone. The I is profoundly influenced by the relationship with the thou.

With each I and with each moment of relationship the I is created anew. When relating to I one holds back something of oneself one inspects it from any possible perspectives one categorises it, analyses it, judges it and decides upon its position in the grand scheme of things but when one relates to a thou one's whole being is involved, nothing can be withheld. Their relationship is an example of an I-It relationship. The therapist sees the young man as a member of an exceptional category, as a prodigy as the new Einstein as a huge potential that needs to be groomed, so that he can contribute to the progress of humanity.

From the first moment he takes him seriously as a person and his whole being is involved in the encounter. He withholds

Transformation

nothing not even his anger and frustration. He is always authentic, transparent and self-revealing in this relationship with the young man and he resists the temptation to diagnose him even when he discusses the young man's past traumas. He uses common words instead of psychological words analytical categories and creates an alliance with the young man's innermost being the part of him that has secretly desired to be discovered. He tries to get beyond the layers of defence mechanisms designed to avoid contact and he is working with the person who is there on the assumption that we exist primarily in a state of relatedness it would be meaningless to distinguish between a real and a transference relationship. This means there is no counter transference only the relationship through which the patient also helps the therapist understand. The restriction of our capacity to keep the world open for what we need and what addresses us can be innate or the result of an unsatisfactory upbringing. It manifests itself in modes of illness which show impairment in our relation to certain intrinsic aspects of being – that is embodiment, spatiality, temporality and mood. All these disturbances encroach on the possibility of realizing the basic ontological nature of human existence, freedom and openness towards other human beings and to all other beings encountered.

What takes place between the two men is a genuine encounter but to what extent is it a liberating one? What must they be liberated from in order to be able to experience greater freedom and openness towards other human beings and what makes it possible for change to occur? In the young man's case his restrictions are his inability to establish any lasting relationships and his abused past. He is suspicious and defensive with whoever he meets. Despite his intellectual capacities he is unwilling to take the necessary steps to fulfil his potential. His problems are related to loving and working. Of the two big Existential themes of the fear of isolation and the need for liberty these are the issues for the young man at this stage. His conflict comes from the fact that he dreads isolation, a fear of being abandoned again as in childhood whilst also craving liberty, taking responsibility and going towards fulfilling his potential and becoming the author of his own life would mean having to face the risk of abandonment.

The key scare is when the therapist tells him that it is not his fault and where he breaks down in tears. This is the moment where he has relations that he can be in the world with other people as he is and still be accepted. He realise that being abandoned is not his fault and that he doesn't need to carry this guilt. His eyes open up to his denial, evasion and distraction techniques and he realises that they are unnecessary. He has been defending himself against the Existential givens.

Chapter 14

The Free Market Existentialist

We philosophers are not afraid of challenges and the need to show that capitalism and Existentialism are compatible and hence a minimal state with a truly free market would be and were the option but there is not just a connection between Existentialism and evolutionary theory, but also the unexpected connection between Existentialism and evolutionary theory.

This is an evolutionary theory that tells us that there are more moral facts, a promise that in turn leads to avowal of the minimal state, which is compatible and conductive to capitalism. To examine each connection in turn, Existentialism highlights individual responsibility over collective action. It is a philosophy which reacts to an apparently absurd and meaningless world by urging individuals to overcome alienation, oppression and despair through freedom and self-creation. The Existentialist living without higher meaning recognizing that anguish and despair are common to us yet all believes in free will.

The Existentialist individual focuses on his or her own choices and struggles ceaselessly to achieve their plans. This is not quite the portrait of Existentialism which is why I devote my second chapter to showing how Sartre's Existential philosophy among others may be compatible with my line of argumentation. I do so primarily through my emphasis on individual liberty. A revisionist outlook is offered suggesting that Sartre's vision of liberty was a hymn to the individual, then the deconstructing the links between that conception of freedom and Marxism. Sartre underwent a philosophical shift because of pro collectivist intellectual fashion spreading widely over Europe during and after the 1940s. His evident belief in autonomy and self-reliance does seem much more suited to free market capitalism than to collectivism besides Existentialism correctly understood might force capitalism to get rid of its nasty perversions such as crass consumerism, greed and the alienation due to unsatisfactory jobs.

Capitalism without consumerism is the promise and good fortune Existentialism can help to define ourselves as individuals and to resist being defined by external forces. In addition in a mere society the Existentialist may be moved by prudence and enlightened self-interest to pursue a kind of voluntary simplicity as an antidote to conspicuous consumption. Prudence and enlightenment self-interest are two main drives for change. Both may be described as long non-moral virtues as there are no such things as moral facts only moral habits shaped by evolution and human interaction. Morality then does not rely on any fixed idea of human nature. Rather, both human nature and morality are fluid and unbounded save by the philosophical limits and if a kind of court morality does exist it is made up of those taboos required for preservation of the species and it is recognized as such all over the world.

Even though occasionally all we can do is override them in some cases when they threatened to curb our legitimate desires. How does the Existentialist deal with this ethical chaos? Quite well because of its emphasis on the authenticity and individual commitment, Existentialism can and should act as a guide for human action. The only standard by which an action can ultimately be judged is can you live with it? If someone objects that the moralism would probably lead to undesirable behaviours is maybe but the overwhelming majority will behave in a way that is best and healthiest for themselves and others. Moral anti-realism, the idea that there are no moral facts here and acts as a bridge between Existentialism and libertarianism.

Trying to reconcile Existentialism, moral anti-realism and the free market libertarianism is a charming idea but not so easy. It required me to build my own picture of the intellectual movement and other philosophers those who love the free market for its tendency to produce greatness. Although I made it clear from the outset that my goal was just to assess whether the set of ideas are well suited some will be left with a sense of scepticism. What is needed is a strategy to reject the commercial world without rejecting the free market and how the free market Existentialist should handle the suggestion that our individual task is to find a way of life that helps us to achieve our chosen purposes.

This of course it is more an exuberant expression of personal taste, preferences and character then a systematic argument. I am more interested in producing a fully-fledged own lifestyle, choices and beliefs than in providing the academic world with a theoretically compelling synthesis.

Chapter 15

Defining Ourselves

We all live our lives in the shadow of other people. Other people feel and to a significant degree constitute our world. After many centuries of history we remain social animals but our identity and its origins remain an issue for us. Although we easily imagine ourselves alone on a desert island we cannot imagine having an identity without having had contact with other human beings. We recognise that other people are shaped by our presence in their lives. We intuitively recognise that other people are a mirror in which we come to see ourselves. Conversely other people are shaped by our presence in their lives. We too are guides, mentors and teachers and on occasion our influence on other people may be a bad one.

Existentialist philosophers over time recognise the influence of other people in the making of oneself. Other people are characterised as an indispensable mediator between ourselves and others. It is arguably the case that we know ourselves largely by what other people say and think about us. Other people become the metric by which we are measured. Yet we often defy such measurement boundaries set by other people who make excellent springboards for a leap into identities not otherwise pursued so whether we embrace or reject what others would have us be we cannot escape the formative influence they have upon us.

Encounters with other people can be a mixed blessing. Failed expectations and miscommunications are frequent. One reason for this is that we understand others only incompletely. The gaps are filled with our imaginings, hopes and fears. Ironically the more we

Transformation

know about others, or others know about us, the more vulnerable we can become. In matters of this sort some Existential philosophers appear to take a very negative stance dramatically emphasizing that the source of much of our discord is the actions, innuendo and words of our fellow human beings.

Aside from the person on person aspect of identity formations, the impact of society on the shaping of individual identity is also key. Dissent from established norms and widely held beliefs remains generally unwelcome by them. Even in a liberal democracy other people want and expect us to resemble them in attitude, appearance and practice. Their displeasure at our departure from the norm is made evident to us in the ways both subtle and overt. However in a truly repressive regime the coercive element becomes decidedly more prominent and the mode of bringing deviants to heel is likely to be violent. This portrays not only the malevolence that can underpin the rule of law but the ordinariness of evil in society.

On the brighter side of human interaction other people can and do help to define us in positive ways. Familiarities and bonds of friendship can inspire interest in mutual welfare. There is a stratagem for facilitating such behaviours in all people regardless of the relationship. It is a therapy for living in an often uncaring world. Its key is how we define and engage others and the notion that solutions must begin with us. First we must recognise and embrace the need for empathy. Next we must avoid treating others as objects as a means for the fulfilment of our self-interests. Lastly to engage with others as simply an end in itself. Albeit a simple and transparent thesis it is worthy of remembering as we encounter others for we may transform each other in ways humanists have long dreamed of.

The ideas of many Existential philosophers continue to inform our understanding of the human condition especially the problems surrounding the social construction of individual identity. Although there are no precise solutions for the human condition in their ideas there are a host of thought provoking ideas many of which are worth reflection even if they are not prescriptive self-help templates. It is inescapable that what people think influences their behaviour so we might all benefit from their ideas with the self-imposed caveat that only our thinking can provide a call to action.

We must also remember that we can never fully get past the biases of our particular place and time. The effect of both nurture and nature will linger in us. Nevertheless we can strive to transcend our present limitations regarding how we define other people. For just as we hear ourselves in the voices of those close to us we in turn echo their voices. By closely the listening to other people's voices we may come to hear their voices in our own.

Art and Music

Chapter 16

An Existentialist View

Singing in choirs. There seems to be that there is a problem that stems from a deep philosophical misconception about the nature of music making and of singing in particular. Humans have been singing since prehistoric times. Singing is not something we need to learn to do. What we need to do is put aside some assumptions both cultural and philosophical which undermine our ability to simply give voice and which makes us believe that we have to make some special effort to do something which is in fact integral to our bodies.

First we often talk as though we sing for effect or to make ourselves and others happy. This implies a utilitarian framework about singing that is done to create some sort of benefit but that way of thinking is simply carelessness. Rather, singing is an expression of who we are, of our own authentic humanity. It is not an add-on for the sake of giving pleasure to ourselves or to others although it may do that as well of course.

This deeper significance is obvious in the context of music in a religious setting. A monk who had been singing as such for decades powerfully explained the significance of singing for him but it is clear that singing is of a much more profound significance than a decorative or utilitarian understanding would imply even for people without a specific spiritual reference. The act of singing is fundamentally person and situation specific. Every singer and every body in which the breath flows and the sound resonates is different from every other. So in this sense there can be no absolute rules for singing. Even the notes we sing are a cultural variant. In Persian and Arabic music, scales include quarter tones whereas in traditional western music there is instead usually an arrangement of semi-tones and toners.

All those rules and principles dreamed up by those whose identity is bound up with such things are relative to their tonal landscape and sometimes irrelevant to the philosophical issues. So rather than trying to generalise about the act of singing let's start from a global concept of singing in which another view towards the specifity of singing. Singing is an Existential matter. That is to say it is not an expression of musical rules or principles. It is not something we do to show how clever or marvellous we are. Rather singing is an expression of our humanity, a humanity which is shared with others and which is therefore most powerful when expressed together with others. When we sing to other people in whatever venue or setting whether a big auditorium or a small gathering we are drawing them into our lives experience.

Being there in whatever context is what matters. Being fully aware of and responsive to the present circumstances. This is a very demanding frame of action or of morality. If we allow ourselves to be diverted from it we will fall short of what we can and even should be. This radical presence in the moment is what distinguishes the professional singers from recreational ones, not their adherence or otherwise to a particular way of singing.

At its best singing is a way of responding often with great flexibility and subtlety to their experience of the world including the sound of other instruments. Although classical music is strictly governed by the written score in vocal all classical music the same at philosophical simplicity of making sound with the body applies. All we can ask of any singer is that they be who they are for us in that moment in time. There is no time or spare intellectual energy for anything else. Indeed anything else, being happy, public approval, even vocal science is a distraction. Of course we can improve the way our voice reflects who we are mostly by clearing away the assumptions and hang ups we have about ourselves and our place in the world.

The breath led sound that's made has a very direct relationship

Transformation

with the embodied self. If what we breathe is what we sing our singing is fundamental to our physical and intellectual space. In the present world moral categories and technical possibilities are changing as fast and so fast we hardly have time to be aware of them let alone respond to them. Perhaps all we can do is give voice. This gives an added urgency to the need for a more nuanced and sensitive atmosphere around choirs and singing groups.

There needs to be a much more thorough awareness of the personal significance of resonating the body to make sung sound. Organisations often talk about the benefits of singing for conditions such as dementia and our health and wellbeing. The focus is on the impact that taking part in the arts can have on health and wellbeing.

What we are talking about is not a utilitarian argument but about a benefit of a different and more basic kind, something more intrinsic to who we are, the value of self-expression for its own sake. Attributed to singing is feeling good but feelings are often temporary reactions to outside stimuli but there is often little understanding of the more radical personal significance of singing. Singing with freedom in the breathing and the use of a resonance will be more compelling to listen to and singing with their own body and being and wholeheartedly being there. It needs to work socially, psychologically and philosophically.

It is a betrayal of our deepest Existential need not to affirm ourselves and our place on this planet. There is still an area of suffering on the boundaries of traditional groups represented by the people who bear the brunt of their philosophical model about the purpose of singing and philosophical clarity in this area would be a wonderful thing.

Chapter 17

Affinity With The Arts

Existential ideas can be framed to affect us in the manner of art. They can arouse intuitions we did not know we had while including passion, pathos, wonder, mystery or fear. This is hardly surprising given what Existential philosophical ideas typically concern, namely our lives and our place within the reality. Neither is it surprising that Existentialist philosophers would cultivate artistic effects to inspire others and to get them thinking. The ultimate aim of this philosophy may be the determination of truth but it can often be an artistic effect that draws us in.

Such effects instigate and sustain philosophical thought and hence do important work not so much in guiding us to the truth as in determining the paths we want to tread and in the minds of truths we want to discover and in motivating and sustaining our search for them. A lecture or text may produce artistic effects in a more or less inspiring way depending on the skill of the philosopher. Artistic effects are neglected in the quasi scientific technical work which dominates today's academic philosophy but they are the mainstay of the history of philosophy. If the philosopher concentrates on producing these effects through music and keeps the actual philosophy to the minimum required to produce them then they might well thus be doing valuable philosophical work, the work that lecturers and texts do when they aimed to produce empathy and engagement in order to inspire reflection. Music moulds, reinforces and shapes our ideas and feelings, most typically love, sadness and passion and it can do the same kinds of things with the

Transformation

more conceptually sophisticated and varied palette of philosophy but a musical rendering also has the advantage that it can aspire to art.

Another advantage to a musical approach is that given its patently artistic aspiration our attention is immediately drawn to the non-argumentative nature of these effects which is something that might pass us by with artistic affection a purely textual treatment. This means that with the use of music in Existential philosophy attention will thereby be drawn to the fact that although we may be moved and inspired we should not necessarily be persuaded. As such the musical performance of philosophy has something in common with the aims of experimental philosophy which among other things provides a check on the use philosophers make of intuitions by empirically investigating a representative sample of a populations intuitions.

The very fact that there is now such a thing as experimental philosophy makes us more wary when we see philosophers appealing to the intuitive high-ground without evidence. Likewise performance philosophy of whatever medium by raising our awareness of the use of non-argumentative effects in philosophy may remind us to keep a level-head whenever these effects are employed, however we may otherwise welcome them.

Chapter 18

Performance Philosophy

Performance philosophy has become a reality in recent years and is spreading fast. It encompasses not only music but also dance, theatre, film and all manner of artistic endeavours which can be inspired by and inspire philosophy. We should welcome this because even though some philosophers like to think of their discipline as a branch of science philosophy has a strong affinity with the arts and this affinity should be celebrated, not hidden away.

This affinity with the arts can immediately be seen from the fact that the history of Existential philosophy is a living part of philosophy in a way in which the history of science could never be part of contemporary science. Philosophy just like an art form has canonical figures whose thoughts have retained their relevance for hundreds even thousands of years. Another reason to welcome the development of performance philosophy is that to be frank, philosophy has an image problem, a pipe and slippers pointless, waffle image problem.

Science is universally taught in schools and breeds celebrities. It pervades our culture and is showered with admiration. Philosophy on the other hand is viewed with suspicion and remains a niche interest outside the stubbornly insular profession itself. This is despite the fact that philosophy is in fact thoroughly ubiquitous. It creeps into blockbuster movies, ground breaking artworks and best-selling novels with surprising frequency. If a novel is acclaimed for its intellectual depth it usually means that it flirted with a little philosophy. Very few apart from the philosophy nerds seemed to notice. So rather than remaining a publicly invisible source for art to draw upon maybe it is time philosophy to start by drawing upon art. Then it could hardly be missed and also might start to be appreciated a bit more. In any case philosophy certainly needs to raise its profile because we are currently on the verge of technological breakthroughs which will bring us to the greatest moral dilemma.

This ethical precipice is most notable in the fields of genetic enhancement and artificial intelligence. If philosophy continues on its current unassuming track then we will soon find ourselves with the anomaly of all the seats on the ethics panel's being taken up by scientists. Philosophy desperately needs more cultural influence and respect for which increased public awareness is a good start. Performance philosophy can help and if you think this will lead to be taken seriously then you are falling back as the unthinking assumptions about levity. In any case when it comes to the big philosophical issues currently facing us is not sure that it could have much less influence than it currently does. We need a great performer. Philosophy deserves it.

Chapter 19

Philosophy And Music

Absurdity and complexity. It is one thing to be both a musician and an Existentialist philosopher but quite another to try to combine them as on the face of it they do not mix. With no evident overlap it seems there could be no good reason to combine music an Existential philosophy. There have already apparently been two good reasons encountered not to try, that the combination seems silly and that music is not an appropriate medium to convey the richness and complexity of Existential philosophical content.

I myself do not think that the first is a good enough reason however and although the second embodies a good point it overlooks a crucial aspect of Existential philosophy.

Firstly to address why it seems silly to present Existential philosophy in musical terms. The reason I think is that Existential philosophy is associated with levity and the result is an absurdity. If a political leader were to deliver a speech about foreign policy say to a disco beat that would be paradigmatically absurd a juxtaposition but then again the same effect could be achieved by hosting a hotdog eating composition sound track of classical music. The reason this switch maintains the absurd effect is that hot dog eating unlike politics is not serious and more pertinently that not all music is associated with levity. Some music is just for fun and can be all the better for it but to assume that all music is so is to make a seriously philistine assumption albeit one it is possibly easy to make until you start to think about it.

The assumption explains one immediate reaction to the idea of

Transformation

singing Existential philosophy. However human beings also have a long track record of producing serious music so if you get the music right I myself see absolutely no reason why a musical setting of Existential philosophical ideas should be absurd so long as there is good reason for it. Setting Existential philosophy to music might put some people off but others might find it focuses the mind. If you think that Existential philosophy is so utterly serious that no music could match its gravity then you probably shouldn't be reading Existential philosophy.

The second reservation is that Existential philosophy is too complex to be effectively conveyed in musical form. I think this is basically but not strictly correct. It is not strictly correct because there is no logical reason why if every single word of a fifty-minute research paper presentation could not be set to music. Very little if any audience interaction transpires during Existential philosophical lectures on the whole but even that could be incorporated if the music had an element of improvisation.

Nevertheless the reservation that Existential philosophy is too complex to effectively convey in musical terms is in practice basically correct because making it happen would require enormous completely impractical amounts of effort for minimal if any rewards. Scoring and rehearsing an Existential philosophical lecture would be a mammoth task so such events could only be occasional one offs reserved for the odd star paper. The clear benefit, for those it did not put off, would be a more entertaining, enjoyable and memorable presentation. The idea would be the same however and they are surely the point of the exercise.

Chapter 20

Existentialism As Punk Philosophy

Existentialism is punk philosophy par excellence. Whenever I am asked so what exactly is Existentialism I experience a sinking feeling. It is a difficult philosophy to explain. Efforts typically end up trivialising or obfuscating so much about it that is important, original and relevant. A number of things account for this but an important one is that Existentialism is a state of mind as much as it is a collection of ideas. The communication of this philosophy benefits from being indirect. To appreciate its significance you have to be there in amongst the detailed stories, rolling critique and inspirational prose. You have to catch a dose of it through its resonance with your own unarticulated fears and aspirations. Along these lines I am offering a new way in, a hook in the form of an analogy. Along these lines with a movement in pop and rock music.

Existentialism I want to claim is the punk rock of philosophy. Punk rock I am characterising as nihilistic, extreme, passionate, liberating, inclusive, amateur and violent. It had precursors and it still exists. In the seventies punk was a wake-up call it was a snarl to an atrophied establishment. It sought to destroy and in the ruins left behind it flexed its gnarly wings and expressed anger and frustration in a crude but deliberate subversion of the previous rock scene. In place of refinement and privilege it offered energy and inclusiveness. The distance between band and audience shrank and sometimes had disappeared. It offered spit, sweat and blood. In place of systems improvable pasts and functional futures it

Transformation

offered an exhilarating and dangerous present like a hyperactive adolescent. It couldn't be staged managed. It wasn't a performance in any conventional sense of the word but a happening. Dada is art that is anti-art. Punk is music that is anti-music and Existentialism is a philosophy that is anti-philosophy.

Punk music is an outside aesthetic but it is still an aesthetic. Likewise Existentialism must recognise a place for reflective rational discourse, since that is necessary to philosophy, but part of its agenda is to identify the limits of such discourse and in so doing redirect us to what this perspective marginalises and represses. It will rail against conceits such as the possibility of absolute knowledge, universal moral codes, an ultimate meaning of life, a final harmony between individual and state and between the self and its possibilities. It will in short point to the limits of rational enquiry and accordingly the limits of the rational minds jurisdiction over a motion, desire and the body. The most radical element of this anti-stance inheres as much in the subversive nature of Existentialisms metaphors and stories as in its theories of the human situation as valid as that theory is.

Punk was a political energy and traded in extremes, songs aggressively delivered. The medium like the message was intense and to the point. Since human existence is so vividly exposed to exploring boundaries, extreme situations present the Existentialist with a perfect method. Punk broke out like a disfiguring rash. It was an attraction repulsion machine and at gig to be spat at that was a compliment. The emotions and minds and moods of the epicentre of Existentialism are anxiety and disgust. Anxiety recognizes the instability and contingency in life and disgust is often maintained as anger and cynicism towards a complacent bourgeoisie who are insensitive to possibility and the fragility of their forms of life. In the grotesque or immoral lurks a strang beauty that corresponds with the unsettling ambivalence that often results from Existential aesthetics.

We refer to authors as Existential as much because of their anti-systematising intensity as for their distinctive ideas. This is not a trivial point. The style models both the fact that only you can know what it's like to be you and the desire to inspire the reader to wake up and take responsibility. My wanting and life is an epigram calculated to make people aware being that Existentialism is a philosophy of action not quietism. We are all philosophers of our own lives. Existentialism is therefore inclusive. Punk attitude is reacting from your own self, your own spirit and not accepting what is supposed to be established. We can all live authentically. Nihilism is that desperate stubborn refusal of the world. It is not an end point but a rite of passage, a temporary descent into the underworld.

Existentialism is not just a reaction against rational or academic excess. It is also something that promotes self-creation and spontaneity. Get life and do something with it. Punk is about a mood that needs full commitment not just appreciation of grooves and tunes but the total attunement of one's rebellious absurd self. It is designed to capture and create adrenalized moments with the escape velocity to inspire life changing self-awareness.

A high proportion of philosophers classed as existentialists have had tenuous relationships with the academic establishments. This doesn't necessarily make their output amateur in the pejorative sense but it does in the sense of placing them outside the establishments. The result can be freedom and spontaneity in their ideas and a perspective on life less biased by the analytical gaze of an academic persona. Also to be on the outside creates a kind of anxiety that focuses thoughts on the concrete content of life as lived. The training and education implies a source of stability which can create a halo that falsifies existence as a whole.

The punk is granted no such illusion. Cult punk spoken word wasn't aiming at like a caress in music but highly unusual spoken word performances. There is good violence against oppression or violence serving as a metaphor for the ostensibly harmless expression of frustration and most of punk is good violence. Some Existentialist philosophers were violent philosophers as they challenge the entire canon of western philosophy and with it the infrastructure of civilised values. But to apply a cultural purgative is to run the risks. By philosophising with a hammer courted misappropriates.

I have here attempted an indirect and partial illumination of the

Transformation

well-known but little understood philosophy that is Existentialism. It is not the whole picture for sure. The punk analogy can't encompass its gentler claims about the mysteries of the human condition and it's more harmonious ties to the academic establishment via phenomenology, hermeneutics psychotherapy and virtue theory. Nevertheless more than any other Western philosophy it's one to be inhaled with keen personal awareness and exhaled in the living moment. For this reason its proper force must be communicated indirectly. Punk was at its most powerful when impossible to define. There is something about vitality that precludes satisfying definitions or manifestos and so all the time Existentialism defies clear categorisation there is reason to believe it's alive and well.

Chapter 21

Relevant Existentialism

There is a general tendency in the non-philosophical world to dismiss Existential philosophy is being purely theoretical with no connection to the type of problems that people are confronted with in their everyday lives but this is not necessarily true. Many Existential philosophers struggled to find ways to improve people's lives by drawing attention to and making people think about fundamental aspects of life. Feeling discontent with the then dominant philosophical system and with every other philosophy Existentialism sought to answer life's questions by trying to show that the only truth that is important is subjective truth.

Only through a deep and honest analysis of oneself can one truly know what one is or is not, what is one's values and beliefs and what are one's truths. No one has a privileged claim to absolute knowledge but each individual can and should think for themselves and so find their own path in life and their own values. This can be done by close examination of one's thinking.

The thing is to find a truth which is a truth for each one of us to find the idea for which we are willing to live and die. What use would it be in this respect if we were to discover a so called objective truth or if we worked our way through the philosophers system? What use would it be in that respect to be able to work out a theory of the state which we ourselves did not inhabit but merely held up for others to see? What use would it be to be able to explain many separate facts if it had no deeper meaning for ourselves and our lives? We must first learn to know ourselves before knowing

Transformation

anything else. Only when we inwardly know and understand ourselves and see the way forward on our path does life acquire repose and meaning.

Each persona is an embodiment of the way of seeing the world, a way of living our life suggesting two main parts of life, the aesthetic and the ethical. The aesthete sees the world through an interesting boring dichotomy when life is made to live, to experience and there are no serious choices. Life is immediacy. For the ethicist, on the contrary there are only serious choices where life is what you make of it. It is not enough to just live it you must make concrete choices that would give shape to your existence, to yourself. Life is responsibility. The ethicist's dichotomy is, let's say, good versus evil. However, although these options look a lot like they represent ultimate solutions they are just possibilities. Neither of them represent an ultimate truth. They are merely choices that one can make in one's life.

The approach however is still relevant because of its focus on the individual. Each of us feels the need for purposes. This purpose can be gained only by our choices, our actions and the way we live our lives. No one can tell us who or what we are or what we should do. We must discover and decide that for ourselves in our innermost intimate place where we can make our true self come to light, then shine upon our own singular path. It is important for us to know ourselves, to discover what are really our values, our beliefs, our truths in order to live a more fulfilling life. It is important to know what we truly are so that nobody can manipulate us into doing what is contrary to our inner selves. It does not present us with absolute truths but challenges us to discover subjective truths for ourselves.

It proposes us to encourage us to discover subjective truths for ourselves to encourage us to become more independent. The phrase know yourself means separate yourself from the other. In the end what it does is dare us to live by choosing how we live and by taking responsibility and rise to expectations.

Chapter 22

Existentialist Ethics

Spoken like a true Existentialist my life is my work. Life and thought are intrinsically linked. We are what we do. Existentialism is a philosophy that outlines the conditions of human existence but rejects any conception of human nature, a philosophy that affirms human freedom but emphasises that it brings with it not happy empowerment but anguish and despair, the philosophy that stresses that humans have choices but experiences little optimism that will make good use of them or even understand what it would mean to make the right choices. It is on this last point that philosophers depart accepting that there is no human nature and that human freedom is absolute that in my situation or any situation whatever we always have choice. In other words human life is not on autopilot nor is there an instruction manual telling us how to make the right decisions.

This means that there is a good deal of ambiguity and in short we must face up to it and live with it. Given this ambiguity there would seem to be a very little opportunity for moral theorising. Not that I object to this standard Existentialist conclusion as we must not expect absolute solutions and lasting answers. We fulfil ourselves in the transitory or not at all but this doesn't mean that all ways of living and courses of action are equally good.

The way forward is to look at the nature of our relationships to other people. Existentialism leads to a clear individualism in which the fact that there are other people presents a constant threat of falling into bad faith. Others judge us and impose limits on us

Transformation

to the unbearable degree that 'hell is other people'. By contrast my own individualism is more nuanced. Is this kind of ethics individualistic or not? Yes if it means by that it accords to the individual an absolute value and recognizes in one alone the power of laying the foundation of one's own existence. The individual is defined only by his relationship to the world and others. His freedom can only be achieved through the freedom of others and here we finally have it. No existence can be validly fulfilled if it is limited to itself. My ethics views the existence of others as an opportunity. In fact it is the only opportunity we have to give reality and meaning to what we do and therefore to what we are. We must invite others to join our projects. Many of us make poor use of our freedom. Some adults still tried to live in the naïve freedom of childhood while others tried to control or manipulate people in an attempt to limit their freedom, a tactic that is ironically doomed to end in self-deception and the limiting of our own freedom.

A mature and constructive use of our freedom our only chance of fulfilling ourselves as individuals involving making a plea to others appealing to them for their attention and cooperation. All our lives are marked by living with others, by ambiguity and freedom. That much is completely unambiguous.

Chapter 23

Existential Hero

The most popular work of the 20th century was written by a man who has not usually been identified as a philosopher but whose work clearly embodies Existential themes. Dashiell Hammatt creator of the hard-boiled detective novels applied an Existential viewpoint to his writing. His novel the Maltese Falcon is an excellent example of literature in which Existential themes run through the story. It begins when a young woman approaches private detective Sam Spade. She wishes him to rescue her sister from a man whom she believes has her sister under his control. He takes on the case but it results in the murder of his detective partner. It also compels Spade into a hunt for a mysterious statue in the shape of a falcon which was allegedly encrusted with jewels. In the end Spade solves the murder of his partner and turns the perpetrator over to the police even though it may ultimately not be in his best interests to do so but Spade says that when a man's partner is murdered he has to do something about it.

Existentialism as defined begins with the premise that existence precedes essence. For many non-Existential philosophers and systems the essence of a person is present at birth. For us existentialists however an individual must define his or her own reality. Because the universe does not provide meaning only existence the Existential task of a human being is to create his or her own meaning and that the central requirement for living a meaningful life is a continual process of self-definites. A person is not defined by what he or she claims to be but rather by his or her activities, and actions.

Existentialists often focus on death in their writings because death provides a temporal limit to the process of self-definition. Existentialists further believed that the defining process encompasses solitude, choice and freedom. In order to create oneself freedom of action is required. Hence one must not become so entangled with the lives of others that one's autonomy is diminished. Generally Existential desires and decisions regarding the creation of self may be difficult ones and can lead to great anguish. Dashiell Hammatt the author, for him and the film Maltese Falcon has Sam Spade the hero of the cosmos is Godless and ruled by chance and violence.

Rather than being in a benevolent universe in which there is progress human beings are alone in a meaningless world. Sam Spade needs to make the point that people do not easily change. Once one has defined oneself it is difficult to become a different person. Hammatt puts it in the novel to make the point that creating one's life requires difficult choices and hard work. Simply leaving one's location does not lead to the creation of a new essence but Sam Spade has defined and is defining himself and this is made clear in the ending of the novel and film.

Sam Spade has finally acquired the elusive Maltese Falcon and he offers to sell it. However the falcon turns out to be a fake and Spade faces a crucial definitional choice. Others join in interested in buying the falcon not knowing it is a fake but Spade refuses to join in even though much wealth is at stake. Instead he calls the police and this leads to their apprehension and arrest. He has defined himself as a detective. Is not only how he makes a living but also who he is.

That definition entails certain behaviour which he cannot change if he is to maintain his identity. Part of being a detective involves catching criminals and bringing them to justice. One's behaviour must meet a standard of universal applicability. One's actions must be applicable to all. Sam Spade has applied this test to his definition of himself as a detective. If all detectives court criminals only to let them go what would be the consequences for law enforcement? Sam Spade's self-definition includes a commitment to doing something when one's partner is killed. It is part of his code as a detective and if he had violated this code he is no longer living within the self-definition he has created and being a detective is who Sam Spade is. In conclusion Dashiell Hammett's, the Maltese Falcon, provides a literary exposition of Existentialism.

His novel continues to be read and studied because unlike many other detective novels of that era, it explores the nature of human life. His work is read because it creates intricate puzzles created for their protagonists to solve and have a bigger philosophical context and as a result of his work will continue to be read and studied by many more generations to come.

Chapter 24

Affirmative Response

Being that degrades itself in the mediocrity of everyday life and of our forgetfulness of existence means we can become so bogged down by the actuality just surviving day by day that we forget to enjoy the knowledge and feeling of being alive in the world. Why is this? Why can we experience moments of an impression and at other times moments of almost divine bliss? And which is correct? Vision or nausea? Meaning or meaningless?

Some view this problem as basically irrelevant. The sense of lack of meaning or purpose is very apparent in literature, philosophy and art. Liberal humanism finds it impossible to accommodate the irrational extremes of human behaviour and stirred up scepticism about whether it is possible to make any absolutely true statement. To add to this is a general sense that certainties have been lost never to be regained or replaced.

Science solves our practical problems but at times only widens the inner void of meaningless. For me Existentialism is a passionate protest against the prevalence of mere cold logic. The basic axioms of Existentialism concern the stature of man. An Existentialist philosopher might commence his analysis of human existence by pointing out that while there are times when a man feels supremely happy and confident and there are other times when he feels substantially less than human. Existentialism offers no consolation it purely confirms the diagnosis that a person must give himself significance because if he doesn't no one else will. The state of mind which refuses to feel at home in a dehumanised world is not just a

20th century phenomena but has its own founding in the work of the poets, artists and writers of the romantic movement and with it man has been repositioned in the universe with the option to obtain what would seem to be ultimate knowledge.

Man is now free to pick the fruit from the tree of knowledge at will. With this newfound freedom in hand the romantics felt that visions of ecstasy and moments of affirmation enabled the introduction of a deeper meaning hidden behind the harsh face of reality. However the plummet back down to cold oppressive reality was at times impossible to stand. It is as if the romantic movement expired in bursts of self-pity. Yet the initial impetus for the centering on the self and the irreconcilable nature of man is nevertheless taken up as a foundation for 21st century Western culture.

Some critics have concluded that the romantic outlook is doomed to failure as it tries to reconcile the irreconcilable. 20th century culture is still eager to achieve this reconciliation. Like romanticism it starts from man and accepts the contradictions within him. Man is both great and helpless with reason and driven by an irrational life force. He cannot give up or withdraw from his earthly effort. He is embarked and engaged in the struggle before he knows there is one. Hence the romantic valuing of the qualities that may see him through, energy, daring, capacity for experience, courage, intellect and imagination.

Given the contradictions inherent in human life it may seem has formed a necessary conclusion in saying that absurdity and nausea were in the norm and however you approach life you are destined to be left empty due to an inability to see beyond ourselves opposed to working through our varying selves with a mind to self-development.

So we are left in flux but with no idea why or which stage of the fluctuation is to be taken as an Existential foundation to build upon. Existentialism is in its essence a confrontation with one's own self and the key question is what's shall we do with our lives? Whatever queries may be levelled against the universe are secondary. The objective of the Existentialist is the salvation of the individual as opposed to a comprehensive intellectual system. Pursuit of a harsh

Transformation

reality is modern men's Existential choice. Alternatively we accept our lot of boredom and triviality and feel that things just happen and thus we are to blame.

Chapter 25

Selfhood

Our lives lack something vital, literally vital, and without this mystical something we are walking corpses so I will try to cut through the jargon to give an idea of what we are missing. We humans are more than mere containment of our bodies and our minds. Our ability to relate to ourselves as mind-body conglomerates, our self-consciousness presents us with our primary task, becoming ourselves. In other words our task is to embrace our self-consciousness by developing a concrete sense of ourselves. That is not as easy as it sounds. Most of us aren't doing so hot.

We can go wrong in a number of ways, four actually. The self is a synthesis of finite and the infinite as well as of necessity and possibility and so can go too far in any of these four directions. The finite and infinite are extremes of imagination. If you get carried away on the wings of imagination you will end up in a fantasy land but if you lack imagination altogether you will become a face in the crowd even to yourself.

Both sides failed to embrace selfhood. Necessity and possibility are extremes of ambition. If you relish the realm of possibility you may end up in a daydream and as a daydreamer, a wish upon a star maker who delegates the actualising of your hopes to fate but if you spend too long kicking the can with necessity you end up either calculating every worldly possibility and probability to discover your future or you again abandon yourself to fate but instead of dreaming you say what will be will be. Both sides again failed to embrace selfhood. So if I have got my head out of the clouds and I

Transformation

am my own person and if I am a realistic dreamer with plans for a good life ahead of me then what's with all the accuratory walking with death business? Hold on. It is not so easy a task becoming a self and if you're defensive that's a good sign you're having trouble. If so you are not alone.

Take for instance the case of the world saver prevalent today. The world saver is eager to save humanity but often forgets that humanity is only a word, a case of infinite imaginative feeling. Or take the scholar who surrounds himself with books and other scholars inside ivory towers whiling away their time in pursuit of worldly knowledge forgetting that our task is in the subject of the self. This is a case of infinite knowledge. Or take the big talker. You have surely met a few who give the impression of dominance and success but masking just dominates impressions, a case of infinite willing. Take for instance the couch potato one of the throng of millions who live it seems to be entertained or take the bureaucrat who day in and day out lives for, even if he gripes about it, the man. Or take the high school student who cannot move unless he has been subsumed into one mob or another, all cases of excess finitude.

Tangentially and remembering that the for the self-undertaking the task of selfhood imagine the horror of the author in the stands of a football match for example hearing the chant we have spirit, yes we do or the elementary school counsellor who insists that anyone can become anything they want to be, excess possibility. Take the religious fundamentalist who preaches ideas that he clings to or anyone who justifies his behaviour on the grounds that 'I am going to do this someday anyway'. They manage to end up in the same camp, excess necessity.

Each of these types and of course each contains its own exceptions. These are just a sample of where our task of becoming a self sails onto the shoals of difficulty but are we right to call these types and you and me the living dead? Or is that accusation a bit of a hyperbole? Perhaps but I also think it is right to show how life can be good without making it look easy. I will take the accusation of deadness in my soul in exchange for the higher standard to which I can look toward a life truly lived.

Chapter 26

Other People And Identity

We live our lives in the shadow of other people. Others fill and to a certain extent and to a significant degree constitute our world. After many centuries of history we remain social animals but our identity and its origins remain an issue for us. Although we can easily imagine ourselves on a desert island we cannot imagine having an identity without having had contact with other human beings. We intuitively recognise that other people are a mirror in which we come to see ourselves. Conversely other people are shaped by our presence in their lives. We too are guides, mentors and teachers and on occasions bad examples for others.

As existentialists we characterise arguably the case that we know ourselves largely by what others say and think about us. We are not funny if silence follows our telling jokes. We are not handsome if most people do not find us attractive. We are not tall if others tower above us. Others become the metric by which we are measured and yet we often defy such measurements. Boundaries set by others make excellent springboards for a leap into identities not otherwise pursued. And so whenever we embrace or reject what others would have us to be we cannot escape the formative influences they have upon us.

Encounters with other people can be a mixed blessing. Failed expectations and miscommunications are frequent. One reason for this is that we understand others only incompletely. The gaps are filled with our imaginings, hopes and fears. Ironically the more we know about others or others know about us the more vulnerable

Transformation

we can become. The source of much of our discord with others is the actions, innuendo and words of our fellow human beings. Aside from the person on person aspect of identity formation, the impact of society on the shaping of individual identity is also key. Descent from established norms and widely held belief remains generally unwelcome by them.

Even in a liberal democracy others want and expect us to resemble them in attitude, appearance and practice. Their displeasure at our departure from the norms is made evident to use in ways both subtle and overt. However it is truly oppressive regimes the coercive element becomes decidedly more pronounced and the mode of bringing it deviants to heel is likely to be vibrant. This portrays not only the malevolence that can underpin the rule of law but the ordinariness of evil in society. On the bright side of human interaction other people can and do help to define us in positive ways. Family ties and bonds of friendship can inspire interest in mutual welfare. There is a stratagem for facilitating such behaviours in all people regardless of the relationship which is a therapy for living in an often uncaring world. Its key is how one defines and engages others and the notions that solutions must begin with us.

First we must recognise that and embrace the need for empathy. Next we must avoid treating others as objects or as a means for the fulfilment of our self-interests. Lastly we should engage with others simply as an end in itself albeit a simple and transparent thesis it is worthy of remembering as we encounter others for we might transform each other in ways humanity has long dreamed of. The ideas of Existentialist philosophers continue to inform our understanding of the human condition especially the problems surrounding the social construction of individual identity.

Although there are no precise solutions for the human condition there are a host of thought provoking ideas worth reflection even if they are not prescriptive self-help templates. It is inescapable that what people think influences their behaviour, that only our own thinking can provide a call to action. However we can never get past the biases of our particular place and time. The effects of nurture and nature will linger on in us. Nevertheless we can strive to transcend our present limitations regarding how we define others. For just as we hear ourselves in the voices of our parents, spouse and friends we in turn echo their voices and by closely listening to all other voices we may come to hear their voices in our own.

Chapter 27

Absurd Coping Strategies

Absurdism is a variant of Existentialism. So what is the absurd? I believed that absurdity means a vast almost comical gap between aspirations and reality. Life itself is absurd because of the chasm between the meaning and the planning we invest in our lives and the mocking indifference of the irrational universe. We cannot fit into the absurdity that surrounds us nor can we escape it. Our absurd situation often compels us to choose inauthentic coping strategies.

The first such coping strategy is that of actual suicide since the absurdity of life begs the question, if the universe is so indifferent to us why not just kill ourselves and get life over with? But to destroy the self is an act of resignation bordering on the cowardly an unseemly giving up when one has the freedom instead to revolt.

The second strategy is that of confronting the absurdity of life is to commit philosophical suicide - the death of our critical thinking characterising philosophical suicide as the stopping up of thinking to avoid uncomfortable thoughts in a scary world. So instead of facing the uncaring universe directly we accept a plausible cover story. Thus various religious and secular doctrines serve to foster hope that somehow the universe cares about our personal fate.

Judaism, Christianity and Islam can each have a palliative effect on the dutiful believer or the same coping strategy might rely on secular belief structure. Religious or secular all such thinking is underpinned by the belief that some higher being or force is at the helm. Such ideas are interpreted such as an exercise in self-deceit. Our escape from the absurd takes us down some strange paths from gangs to consumer culture we are replete with escape strategies but such solace affords only a temporary respite from the icy indifferent states of the universe.

Philosophical suicide of the religious type is found within the many writings all testify to life's absurdity but they diverge on an important matter. To some there is something far greater than worldly existence, a belief in God to which rationality does not fully apply whereas others the meaningless is make meaningful by way of revolt.

A laugh is the easiest answer to all that is strange in this life and this attitude is a revolt against life's absurdity. It may provide us with a royal road to an exhilarating sense of freedom. No longer bound by the prospect of thought stopping philosophical suicide we revolt not only to avoid the absurdity but to embrace it. Succinctly put we must be happy with our friends, in harmony with the world and earn ourselves happiness by following a path which nevertheless leads to death. This leaves us no easy answers to the issues we confront.

Chapter 28

Subject To Criticism

Ethical subjectivism is the idea that there are no universal moral standards or criteria and that moral judgements such as right and wrong are based merely on an individual opinion. Examining the question of subjectivism we first look at the charge as it applies to Existentialism in general and then investigate whether or not it applies to ethics of ambiguity.

The first subjectivist charge against Existentialism ethics is that Existentialism bases ethics on freedom it offers no criterion with which to distinguish right and wrong actions but the ethics of ambiguity are not undermined by this objection, because it does offer criteria for distinguishing between actions that are moral and those that are not. These criteria are firstly that we must not engage in a bad faith or self-deception and secondly that we must act to defend and develop the moral freedoms of our self and others.

We hold that humans are ontologically free but that doesn't mean that anything goes. Given that Existentialisms credo is that values and the creation of human freedom and criterion that can be used to distinguish wrong actions from right sections is subjective. Freedom is the source from which all significations and all values spring. It is the original condition of all justification of existence.

Although this statement is consistent with implications that more judgements are subjective this concept applies to the notion of moral freedom which is to will oneself free and accept the responsibilities this choice entails. So with our freedom we create values but underlying this subjectivity is an objective morality of freedom. So an additional question arises of how one can know if any given action does lead us in the direction of more freedom. However we do not always know what the results of our choices will be as a future into which we project ourselves has not yet happened. Therefore we can never really know if we are making the right decision.

We may not know the outcome of a given choice or action and it is safe to say that consequences are there when we reject the utilitarian approach to making ethical decisions. Even though we don't know what the specific outcome of a choice will be we can estimate whether we are making the choice to will our or another's freedom this being the criterion for acting in moral freedom. We make the right choices when we acknowledge the other. The world is disclosed to humans through humans and so meaning arises out of intersubjectivity not in isolation. Therefore the ethics of ambiguity could be understood as being an ethics of care.

The ambiguity of ethics of recognizing others freedom is a response to the ethical needs of others as well as one's own ethical needs. The ambiguity of the human condition suggests that the relationships between self and the other like the relationships between the material and the transcendent aspects of our being is one of reciprocity to will oneself free is also to will others free. This gives rise to the possibility of moral obligation and also moral freedom.

Since the individual is defined only by his relationship to the world and to other individuals he exists only by a transcending himself and his freedom can only be achieved through the freedom of others. Meaning and the world are both disclosed through humans and so full freedom, even in our own activity can only be preserved in our free actions when we work to advance moral freedom classified as merely subjective of the self is intersubjective and relational in its freedom.

This full freedom even in our own activity can only be preserved in our free actions when we work to advance and preserve the freedom of others otherwise we cannot disclose freedom to ourselves. It suggests the conception of the self is self as relation and the ethics of ambiguity are objective and partly based on the care that is concern for others freedom and once again this provides objective criteria for determining whether or not a choice or action is moral. There is no such thing as an isolated individual.

Chapter 29

Autonomy

Perhaps many people do seem to be largely the product of their environments and biological inheritance but I could argue that whatever the term greatness means it is usually manifested by those who have exercised their autonomy to a considerable degree to significantly free themselves from external influences in true Existentialist manner.

These are usually people who have used their strong willpower to harness their autonomy and self-discipline to expand themselves and develop a high level of skill and expertise to actualised their innate potential and to become more than the sum of their influences. In a sense this is only an extension of what every human being ideally does as they move from childhood to adulthood to develop more self-control and autonomy.

As we move through childhood we begin to control our impulses and desires. For example we learn that we can't have everything exactly when we want it and so learn to delay gratification developing self-control. As we need less care and attention we exercise more autonomy, learn to make more decisions for ourselves and to follow our own interests and goals. In this sense human development is a process of becoming less bound by a biological and environmental influences and gain more free will and autonomy. Ideally this process should continue throughout our lives.

Spiritual development can also be seen as a process of gaining increased autonomy. For example many spiritual traditions place great emphasis on self-discipline and self-control of our own behaviour so that we no longer cause harm to others, control our desires so that we no longer lust after physical pleasures, control our thoughts so that we can quieten the mind.

In some traditions spiritual development is seen as a process of taming the body and mind through intense self-discipline requiring self-control. Although it can suddenly and spontaneously the intense awareness is usually the culmination of increasing our innate quotient of personal freedom to the point where our minds become the dominant influence and we become master of ourselves.

Existential philosophers mean something familiar with the concept of self-overcoming. Human nature is not fixed or finished. Human beings are part of an evolutionary process. The potential for human beings is not self-satisfaction but who has the urge to overcome themselves. We all possess a degree of freedom and we all have the capacity to extend the degree of freedom we're bequeathed, to be less dominated by our genes and brain chemistry and the society and environment into which we are born.

We are all potentially much more powerful than we are led to believe even to the extent of being able to alter or even control the forces that have been supposed to completely control us. To a large extent our wellbeing, our achievements and our sense of meaning in life depends on this. The more we exercise and increase our freedom the more meaningful and fulfilling life will be. The most important tasks of our lives is to develop more free will and autonomy. In fact a primary way to develop positivity and begin to live more meaningfully is to transcend the influences of our environment to become more oriented towards who we authentically are.

We have innate potentials and characteristics that are independent of external factors even if this aspect of us may be so obscured from us that we can barely see it. Our task is to allow that part of us to express itself more fully which often means overriding adverse cultural and social influences. We can resist influences to control and even remould our behaviour. It is by no means easy but we can overcome our programming. We don't have to blindly follow the environmental and genetic instructions we were born with. We can increase the quotient of autonomy with which we were born.

Human beings are the only beings who have the power to ignore the dictates of their genes. Our everyday experience is that there are always a variety of choices of thoughts and actions in front of us and we feel we have the freedom to choose any of them and to change our minds at any point no matter what social and environmental forces influence us we are here and can make our own decisions in how we react to the world. Our free will is one of the strongest features of the self

Existentialist philosophy emphasises the human autonomy asserting that choice is one of the defining characteristics of human life. The sheer extent of our freedom may induce a state of disorientation and dread and we make our choices in fear and trembling but the freedom to choose courses of action without fully controlling or even knowing their consequences contributed to human anxiety and human behaviour is not necessarily determined by our past and present experiences since we always have the capacity to make choices based on our assessment of current situations.

Chapter 30

Two Ways

There are two ways of doing philosophy. The first is perhaps close to what most people think of when they hear the word philosophy, today and that is arid, obscure and disconnected. Not that they particularly care. Academic philosophy itself is arguably responsible for this indifference. Many professionals feel or act as if philosophies time is up, in a sense real intellectual advances are now the work of science.

Philosophy has handed over responsibility for subjects that used to fall within the remit of philosophy like physics and psychology. All that is left for philosophy to do now is provide a bit of intellectual scaffolding to support the great empirical edifice as required and are happy to do so. Philosophy has become scientistic in the sense of borrowing it's self-image from science saying that its ambition enough to be employed as an under labour. This means clearing the ground a little and removing some of the rubbish that lies in the way of knowledge. However there is a second kind of philosophy too, the Existentialist sort which is nothing short of a way of life.

For wonderful questions occupy human beings right through their lives. Arguably that makes us human. Existential philosophy develops as life deepens and this philosophy is not just a series of technical discussions, interesting thought experiments or even a way of tackling moral problems though it is partly these things. It is fundamentally a desire to see more clearly and thereby live more fully. When that is coupled to the pursuit of the good and the transcendent, a notion philosophers have only flinched from relatively recently in the history of the subject, this philosophy might be called a spiritual exercise. It is an invitation to transform yourself and in that sense it is an art.

What is Existential philosophy about at heart? Not the virtues of rigour and coherence for their own sakes, but enlightenment. As a way of life thought is therapy. It is a question of struggling with our passion. The feelings that fly about in all directions and are the key source of suffering. The aim is to nurture enjoyment of life in contrast to worrying about it. We all seek tranquillity born of knowing what really gives us pleasure. It is also about cultivating attention and being aware of what is happening in the present moment. We value personal choice and intellectual freedom yet to some the suggestion that Existential philosophy might make us a better human being seems close to a dictatorial.

Another concern might be that such visions of philosophy blurs the boundaries with self-help and anxiety arguably exasperated by the possibility that self-help has grown to fill the vacuum created by the move of philosophy to the cultural side lines. Existential philosophy increases humanities understanding of itself which is a hallmark of a humanistic discipline. The value of Existential philosophy ultimately lies in how it changes us and at its best it introduces us to conceptions of what is possible and way beyond ourselves. Its questions enlarge our conception of what is possible, enriches our intellectual imagination and diminishes the dogmatic assurance which closes the mind. When Existential philosophy becomes less desiccated it returns to its lifeblood, life itself. The aim is to be personal and polarised and to be on the right way to live. Being an Existentialist philosopher is to live the examined life assaying and / or explaining.

In Conclusion

Existential Philosophy Matters

Nobody does research except in the hope that it may at some point make some difference but that difference is often not simply a matter of economic benefit or gain.

For instance the impact of Existential philosophy and its research is to say the impact of the absence of Existential philosophy research often shows when social, political and cultural life runs aground because people are seeking a set of goals, norms or standards that cannot be jointly satisfied.

For example when people demand equal access to status conferring goods (prizes for all) meritocratic processes with egalitarian outcomes, freedom of choice with complete security and many other impossible combinations.

Understanding why we cannot have it all and which changes are possible are often philosophical tasks and there is philosophical work to be done whenever people, institutions or government's find themselves with incompatible aims and standards. So Existential philosophy matters.

We cannot be prescriptive about the channels through which will change the world but we can see that changes won't happen if we hoard philosophical research in obscure academic journals.

We have to engage with others. To some it seems burdensome but from the Existentialist philosophers point of view wider discussions often lead to new understandings for all.

Experiences differ but mine has always being that philosophy and philosophers contributions are neither negligible nor useless and also that taking part in wider debates may alter the view of the weight and point of their philosophical arguments. Existentialists put a fundamental emphasis on unique self and subjective experience.